Chapter 1
About My Past

My name is Lyndsey Horncastle I was born into a loving family, comprising of my parents Mark and Wendy, sister Kimberley and brother Carl. There were not much differences in our ages so family life was busy. Mum was a housewife dad a police officer, often working day, nights and any overtime going. From birth onwards my parents and I faced many visits to various health professions for speech therapy, eye tests various screening procedures.

I've lost people I love and adore even before I was born. I've lost my uncle which was my dad's and the family's brother to brain tumour and that was before I was born; he was only 15 years old in 1982. I didn't really know him but I spoke to my dad about my uncle and he told me what he likes to do and even what his favourite sports was.

When I was born although it was 2 weeks early you weighed 4lb 4oz. From me being born I was under the hospital for my heart condition. The nurses wrapped you in foil to keep you warm. All you could see was 2 big eyes. You looked like E.T. Getting clothes your size was very hard Nannan Nichols knitted you some dolls clothes ie little cardigans to fit you. Everything else was to big.

You went on your first holiday to Bridlington when you were about 8 weeks old. We went with Nannan and Grandad Biggin. You started crawling when you was about 8 months old. You used to pull yourself along with your arms with your tummy still touching the floor (commando style) very funny. As i got older you was very mischievous. When you started walking you used to try and climb out of my cot, sometimes you were successful. When you went onto solid food you never liked eating meat I used to spit it out. We tried everything to camouflage it but nothing work. I also had my injections. Both Nannan and Grandads came to visit me in hospital the rest of the family waited to mum, dad and I was home and everyone had cuddles. I had a cuddle with Grandad Biggin I looked into his eyes. I also had a cuddle with Nannan Nichols and I was looking into her eyes too with Grandad Nichols looking and smiling. I had the award for the most hats worn in a year. 1st winter all dressed up to be the first baby on a mission to the North pole. 1st Birthday I went near the tv and wounded what the fuss was about. I also stuck my head in the washing machine I don't know why. I have I photos taking when I was playing with my toys. I also went to the park had a photo taken and somebody push me! My 2nd attempt to the North pole, with a new recruit. I also got a photo when I had sunglasses on inside who turned the lights out?! Then my sister was born I have a photo of dad mum, me and Kimberley I also had a shoulder ride with Grandad Nichols I went to Nanna and Grandad Nichols house and I was in the back garden and I had a practice run for first trip to the seaside! We did have photos when we went to Skegness on a family holiday. Unfortunately we had no photos as I un-ravelled the film from the camera! At 18 months old I had to were Glasses apparently I was going near the TV. When I was very young by accident trapped my sisters fingers in the door it was when we was living in Eckington. When me and my sisters was growing up we had a gate with a gab in it and I got though it to go out with my sister apparently we was going to the pub! I went to see the doctors for my speech therapy. I had my injections Hepatits B, Pole, injections. Then my brother was born we had photos taken and we had to move house because it wasn't big enough so we moved house into our new place and I was riding my bike with stabilizers on in the back garden. We had a guitar dads music has taken a toll on me. Then when it was nice, we had the paddling pool out in the back garden. Me, Kimberley and Carl went in it. We all went to see some Tractors and cars (not just any cars they are Chitty Chitty Bang Bang) for the day, I also went on motorbikes with bumpers on them and when I was a little older we went to the pub which was Yellow Lion it's a family pub were everyone can go and enjoy them self's. I also did

Brownies and Guides We went to the park when it was nice were we was growing up. And I did swimming lessons at Aston comp and my life saving. We also went to see my uncle's when we were younger to visit them and to see how they were. And we went to see Nannan & Grandad Biggin to see how they were and had a chat with them and if it was nice we went to the park they also had a dog we was playing in the back garden with her and she was having a rest in the back garden. And we also went over to see Nannan & Grandad Nichols to see how they were too and if it was nice we went in the back garden and played games which was garden balls, swing ball, swing. We pretended to be by the seaside. We stayed over for the weekend and had biscuits in bed has Grandad Nichols went down stairs to get them, then we got ready to go down stairs to have our breakfast then we went outside there was a swing in their back garden and garden balls which we did outside and woodwork which was outside they had a little shed which was woodwork. My grandad had his own plants in his garden which he was growing his own vegetables. I also had a tamagoyaki and a furby. And I had a secret Diary.

I had my moments when I was younger it was sometimes stressful for my mum. My sister and brother had wait for me to finish my tea has I was the slowest eater. We had family round at a weekend to see how we was and we was playing

games inside with our cousins. And than another weekend we went out to the pub with our family and my dad friends has well. Went to Nannan and Grandad Biggin the family was there and they had wigs I but one on me. I've got a photo of me wearing one. We also had a type righter which was back in the old days which I had a go on.
I was In a bad relationship that's why I'm obviously I'm not holding back…

I had to go to Meadowhall to get my eyes checked yearly.
Obviously I had open heart surgery done twice because the first time it didn't work. Which we had to go and see them yearly first at the Sheffield children's hospital and then later on at the Northern General Hospital and
then I had my surgery done at Leeds General Hospital.

Chapter 2

I went to nursery and I met new people and made a lot of new friends we was playing together has you do. I also had a best friend in nursery.

Then I went to Aston Hall J & I School and I got my Record of Achievement Class Y1P School Year 1991-92 Year 1 Key Stage 1 English I've done speaking and listening activities and prolonged writing sessions. And I enjoy particularly enjoys role- play situations. Mathematics Able to count, count, read, write and order most of her numbers to ten. Science, Technology (Design and Technology, Information Technology, Geography, History, Art, Music, Physical Education, Religious Education and Personal Development (including other achievements and experiences of the pupil in the life of the school). class Y2A School Year 1992-93 Year 2 Key Stage 1 Personal Development has been good and has more coordinated and has greater control over herself and objects and working independently and goes to the correct task., Y3G 1993-94 year 3 Key Stage 2 Personal Development including other achievements and experiences of the pupil in the life of the school, I am a very friendly nature and is always so chirpy and full of energy. And was doing English, maths, history, geography Technology, Mathematics, Physical Education Art and Religious Education. We went to my Auntie and Uncle's wedding it was day and night and all the family was there. Me and my uncle was having a chat and he told me why I was getting goosebumps also getting chills up my spin and down again, it's because I have presents with him I don't know why I've got them. I didn't ask when I was talking to him. I was in shock when I found out. I wished I had found out why I've got them but

I was too young to understand at that age. Class Y5A School Year 1995-96 year 5 Key Stage 2 Personal Development I have made a lot of progress in many areas. I have had full of enthusiasm and self confidence. Also I have work incredible hard and always tries my best. I am always helpful in class and polite. I am we behaved. English Mathematics geography history Art Technology (Design and Technology, Information Technology, music Physical Education Religious Education I had a record for music, PE and when I was doing maths I had a support teacher and for reading. I also went out to a store with the headmaster and I had a go on the harp. When I was at school I was playing in the playground and doing games and sports when it was summer.

My medical is ASD -surgically closed-2003 but open up again had it done in 2007. Repeat surgical ASD repair for dehiscence of patch. ECG sinus rhythm-August 2012. Echo-July 2012- no residual ASD shunt. Small area of thinning in membranous septum- no evidence of VSD. I've also had check ups for screening for cancer.

We went to Yellow Lion pub there was a ball pool upstairs and some games upstairs but when I was putting my shoes away the shoe rack fell on my little toe I was crying my eyes out I went down stairs and I was crying my eyes out and I was sat on my dad's lap to calm myself down.

I did a Victoria Day where we had to dress up has Victorias and we went to war and learnt about it.

I was doing PE there was a ladder and I tried to walk on it but I slipped and did my chin there was blood all over the place and I had to go to hospital and I had butterflies' stitches.

We had our Christmas dinner and our Christmas concerts too and I was Mary one of them. We also did plays too.

We had a pet Hamster and it was called Woggle we all had to taken it in turns to wash his cage out and one day when I was 10yrs old when he died. I was shocked and also Queen died too. I've also got a sister and a brother I'm the oldest one. We was playing in the back garden and we also had rollerblades when I was younger don't know why because I still kept falling over and did my chin; and again I had a plaster on it. At the weekend I was playing in the garden; When it was nice weather, and when it was raining, I was watching TV.. I was also in a football match playing for Aston Hall Junior & Infant school. Also I was playing with my friends I didn't have a boyfriend then but that's ok as I was fine on my own, when it was summer. I did games which I enjoyed doing and sports day until my last year at Aston Hall Junior and Infant School.

I had to go to the staff room I think my ear was blocked then and I totally messed it up I said resources room for my headmaster. I had a party which I had no clue about the party it was a surprise for me which it was all quiet my mum and dad was there. I got presents and cards saying good luck in your new school which was Abbey School which I was going to; I was 10yrs old then. Record of Achievement School Year 1996/97 Class 6 school Year 6 Key Stage 2 . English, Maths, Science, Technology and Information Technology, Geography, History, Art, Music, P.E, R.E, Personal Development, Class 3 Year 9 Key Stage 3 School Year 1999/2000. English, Maths Science, History, Geography, Modern Language Information Technology Design Technology, Art, Music, R.E, P.E, Swimming. Class 2 Schoolyear 2000/01 10 Key Stage 4 Communications, Numeracy, Science, MFL, IT, When I left there and started my new school I was 11yrs old at school. I got bullied the first day at school, I cried and had to go to the headmaster office. And they all had to say they was sorry but it didn't stop there, they started again and I cried on my way home and my mum and dad saw me when I was upset, so my dad had to wrote a letter to the

Chapter 3

headmaster before he went to work, he did it on the computer without seeing the keyboard which I wanted to learn, and I had to give it to him the next day when I went to school. I was also shy when I was new I didn't know anyone there until I got used to them and I started making friends with them. A boy was looking at me when I started I was sat on a beach. And I was doing to same. I also fancied a boy there I didn't tell him I waited to Valentines Day, which was 14th February to get the card, at the weekend with my mum. My mum was a housewife and I had to wait for my taxi which was on time and sometimes late; Normal it's late. The next day it was Valentines Day I went to school and gave it to him he also gave me a card but it was line paper, but it was nice of him to do that. I didn't expect it and that was it we was boyfriend and girlfriend…. Of course it didn't stop there my boyfriend was also getting bullied at school and I was trying to calm him down. He was playing football or cricket at break time or at lunch time, I didn't mind because I was with my friends, One day he didn't play football or cricket and he stayed with me and our friends, we were playing true dare double dare kiss command or promise. I also wanted to get my confidence back and start sticking up for myself.

I also went back to Aston Hall Junior & Infant School because my friends what was still there did a alphabetical order that they had to read out which I joined in.

On Christmas Day we went to the Cemetery to see my uncle and sometimes but flowers on to respect him. I wish he was here so I can talk to him we have a photo of him so I can just look at him and think of him. We had Christmas dinner at my Auntie and Uncle house and after we all played games and had a laugh and then we had tea and went home. When me Kimberley and Carl went out when we was kids we went to a pantomime with Nannan and Grandad Biggin we meet them there and they was playing Bingo. And on Boxing Day we all went to Nannan and Grandad Biggin house we was playing game's as you do also my Nannan and my Auntie did sandwiches for us we even saw my dad's mates which we said hello to them sometimes they came in and sometimes they didn't. When they came in they said hello and we said hello back. My dad and Grandad went out with their mates. My uncle came with his mates he was outside I didn't recognise him at first but when I said what was up with him I did have a drink of water because I was hot. I had goosebumps and I knew who he was. it was my uncle who I have presence with I have chills going up my spine, I honestly don't know why it happens. We went to bed and I was in the back bedroom he throw some stones up I did say to be quite because my sister was asleep but it didn't wake her he did say sorry and I said its ok. I did want contact with him I was still young at that point and I did cry when he was there also I said I love him which he's family and when he lefted but I knew I didn't have a mobile. And then we stayed over for the night and when it was morning I cried again I wished I had a hug from him because it makes me happy to see him. And we went back in the morning.

Also I support Sheffield Wednesday football club which it's short for UTO'S. I went to the football games in Hillsborough there was a shop next to the football filed with my dad when I was younger. We also went to see my uncle also a godfather and Auntie to see how they were they had cats. I was also a bridesmaid with my sister and two other girls who my Auntie's and uncle knows that was a day and night which was good and to see all the family and my Auntie's side of the family. Me and my sister Kimberley went to see Blue which was a boy Band and then we went to a Wedding reception I also had goosebumps there as well I didn't see him though which was good to see ever one and that was my mum's side of the family.

Then anther weekend me and my sister went to see Spice Girls it was a good night with our Auntie and her friend's then we stayed at my Aunties and uncles I also had goosebumps there and I didn't see him I was indoors we both stayed at there's until the next day.

Also I went to my friend's house not that far from Meadowhall. It was my friend's birthday.

We also played badminton in the back garden. When it was nice and we also had a slide in the garden.

We had a barbecue in the back garden with friends and had a basketball net and we was playing until it was time for tea. We had to be careful because of the barbecue was lit. And also we had a game of cricket in the back garden. My dad had his exercising stuff in the garage.

In 1998 we went to Butlin's for the day and I was watching wrestling there it was in a building and they are three Undertakers ones got purple gloves on and two have grey gloves on one with the purple gloves on was in the pavilion inside it was amazing and I've never have seen it before. I didn't have a book who was coming out and it was my favourite wrestler the Undertaker he did the same moves has the one in American which he won. If I had more time I would have got an autograph and told him he his amazing. I had goosebumps when he came on he was amazing. Wish I had his autograph and picture with him to remember him that will always be a memory to me. I will always remember him no matter what happens weather he's retired or still wrestling.

We also went on holiday to Turkey one year with our friends who we knew, we all was having fun in the pool and diving in the water and at night time we was having a dance and having a giggle. And another year we went to Greece for a holiday that was good too. I enjoyed myself it was all about having fun and meeting new people. Which I sure did.

At Abbey School I did Key Stage 4 programme accredited by City and Guilds and AQA. At Rotherham College of Arts and Technology has an introduction to further education. I've had the opportunity to study the following case studies: in Health and Social care. I've done food for Health, living an Active life, Leisure and Recreation, Drug use and Abuse, Sex Education, Relationships, Health and Safety for All, Planning Diets, Preparing for Employment, Construction(RCAT), Design and Make Project's, Outdoor, Budgeting, Learning about Islam and Christianity, Science 1 (RCAT) ,Science 2 (RCAT), Solar System, Energy and Safety in the Home, Digestion, Art, Design Craft Techniques, French Y10, French Y11,

Citizenship, Public Transport, CAM/CAM(RCAT), Catering1(RCAT) Catering2(RCAT). And I did

Chapter 4

catering which I enjoyed I even prepared and cooked the food. I went to North Yorkshire Moors Camp that was Monday 15th – Friday 18th June 1999 with my friends I even did a tent with my friends we had to do it in teams. I also went to Whitby, Eden Camp, Scarborough, Dalby Forest when we arrived. I had fun and doing lots of stuff what you learn about cooking and cleaning and learning about doing a fire with rocks to light it up which was ok but sometimes stress full at times. I also did rock climbing without a harness and with a harness. I had fun like a normal girl should with your friends.

About 1998 I did Martial Arts (Karate) which is self-defence and I have not used it on anybody which I enjoyed doing and I got more confidence in me it is hard but it's good to make new friends and know how to defend yourself. You get different coloured belts and certificates when you pass. I've also got a photo of my belts.

I even served the food in the restaurant one evening for my family and that was nervous but I didn't think of it and that was 2000-2001. I've also done a young sailors Certificate, Basic Course in French, Sports Captain, another Certificate for Swimming, 2 Essential Skills award, e2e, BT Swimming selection 1,2 and 3, Rotherham MBC in south Yorkshire Youth Games-Swimming, anther Swimming Certificate for competing at the B.T Disport/ D.S.E. Junior Swimming Gala at Ponds Forge I.S.C., Sheffield. Another Swimming Challenge Bronze in 98 and Gold in 97. I also got a Certificate for BT Football Bronze Award. I also got certificate Silver 1 Star and Silver 2 Star I had to get merits before I had my certificates. Me and my friends went to Rotherham Festival of Gymnastics & Dance.

When the Dance finished me and my family went to the Yellow Lion pub and meet our friends there who we know. I had goosebumps when I went passed I knew who it was I should have said hello to my uncle which when I came back down and there was another sitting area I went up there and my uncle was gone. I had that chance to say hello but has long has he's ok and looking after himself that all that matters, and I went upstairs there's another room which I watch wrestling and it was Friday night raw which its WAR is RAW which it is WWF which stands for World Wrestling Federation and its great. I told my dad that I was watching it and he was saying its fake my uncle was down were there's another bar area I told him it's not but that's my dad opinion. I went to the toilet and my uncle said are you ok I said I'm fine thank you I didn't give him a hug but I knew I was fine with goosebumps and chills going up my spine. One night we went to the pub and I went outside on the monkey bars and I did it all the way to the other side of the area and back again and I did it I was so proud of myself for doing it. Nobody was there to distracted me I wished my uncle was there he would have been so proud of me for doing it I haven't done it in ages though. They also did a quiz night there my dad was the quiz master he read the questions out and then he had a break and read the answers out I think they was 10 or more I was still young I wasn't allowed in the bar area until I was 18 that's when I was allowed to drink alcohol.

I also played football for Abbey School it was an away game with my friends we did lose but I enjoyed myself.
Me, dad, brother and sister all went for a bike ride that was exhausting but I enjoyed it because it was fresh air and my legs was hurting but a good hurt not a bad one. We went down a path way before you get to Aston Hall J & I School then there woods on your left side that's were you can go down and there was anther path were you can go fishing but you have to be quite that's the way we went, then we got on to the main road and we

went home and that was a long bike ride but good exercise.

I went on my bike on my own but not a bike ride I went anther way then went across the park I had goosebumps on my arm but I didn't take no interest of what it was then I relies it was my uncles presents again but didn't say anything I just went home I still had that chance to say hello but I didn't. I wished I did but didn't know how to. I also went to the cricket club in Aston. I also had goosebumps I walked round the cricket pitch and I knew when he drove passed I knew who it was but he didn't say hello but it would have been nice to see how he was but he looks well without him saying anything to me that was in the afternoon, and we went there at night time and we had a game of cricket and I went goosebumps again I was the bowler and then I had a go at the bat and I still had goosebumps I knew who it was but my uncle didn't say hello. My uncle properly didn't want to talk but that's ok I'm not going to force him. I didn't say anything but I knew who it was straight away but he didn't talk because he was in the car but that's ok.

I also watch wrestling on TV at the weekend because I like it, And my favourite WWF/WWE

Superstar is the Undertaker he gave me goosebumps when he came on. It does say Please do not try this at home!

Chapter 5

I also climbed trees when I was younger near Aston Hall J & I School there was woods near the school. I climbed up the tree but then I thought "how do I get back down" so I looked down and started getting headache so I looked back up and I put 1 leg down and then the other leg down and so on. Also when I was younger we was playing in the garden water balloons my sister wasn't happy so it was just me and my brother I chased my brother up the drive way and got it on the chest where my scar is, it was hurting me and we finished it there. I also did other things there has well. I missed break time and lessons so when I was 16yrs old I left school I didn't see my first boyfriend from school I went to a different college which was Dinnington and we went into a classroom we all had to introduce ourselves I was quite but I know one person wasn't quite at first but I also got to know people and it was funny. I met someone else in 2002, it was my ex partner I thought he was nice and respected me. We change numbers but he was very quiet he didn't tell me why he wasn't happy he was always very grumpy all the time. It was a toxic relationship the minute I had the letter he had no respect at all that's when I knew I was a down fall and I had no control I also couldn't do PE because it supposed to be the operation on my heart before I left school but the hole was to big but I still went to support my friends I had a letter to prove it.

My ex partner didn't appreciate that I couldn't do PE in Herring Thorpe Leisure Centre it was badminton where I did my dance and also you can do Basketball, Rock Climbing and Swimming there. I had a letter providing it but still didn't believe me when he saw the letter he didn't play because he wanted me to play but I said I can't, it was hurting a bit when I left school until I had another letter from the hospital to get the all clear. Went back to Rotherham Herring Thrope Leisure Centre and I did PE I did Rock Climbing I had the all clear but my ex partner didn't want me to do it but still did Which I tried to get to the top but couldn't my ex partner didn't appreciate that either but he wanted me to get back into a routine in Badminton. I was taking my time because I knew I had to get myself back into games my friends was there to support me they asked me to see if I was alright and I said yes they was doing it quicker then me but I knew I had to take my time. I didn't get to the top I only got halfway I did have a go but I was in a harnesses to protect me, I could hear my friends having a laugh and joke but that didn't

stop me there they was cheering me on apart
from my ex partner who was laying on the Blue
mat. When we finished for the day "he told me I
should not have done it" but I wanted to
because if I hadn't and had a letter he would
not be happy. He thought he was in control of
me but he also told me that I had to do what
he says and I said "you don't control me or
owe me "if I want to do something I will. But still
didn't listen to a word he said. So I had a go
my heart was hurting a bit but I was taking my
Time when we finished I did hold my heart but
My ex partner wasn't at all happy with that."
He said it served you right" it was my decision not
yours you don't owe me. He was very
Manipulative and controlling I knew I had to get out
of it but I couldn't I felt trapped inside of me
he didn't respect me at all. And I said if I had a
letter for not doing it you wouldn't be happy
"you don't control me" because I was getting
my routine back my ex partner wasn't happy then
either but when I was laughing with my friends
he wasn't happy at all. He also saw me
laughing too he didn't like it when I was
laughing with them and he did the spear what
Goldberg did but didn't spear me as you can't
do any of their moves because he's not a
professional wrestler.
We all went to Meadowhall for the day I wanted to
go with my friends but my ex partner stopped me

from doing that we were holding hands he squeezing them so I couldn't get my hand out I did cry a bit because I can't have fun. I had to choose between them or him he keeps thinking he's in control of me when he's not. I had to choose between them or him he keeps thinking he's in control when he's not he told me that I have to do has he said all I was thinking is my friends having fun you don't control me" back to the minibus I saw him holding hands with someone else which he was two timing me because I have a scar on my chest, so he's disrespectful to me and Grandad Biggin when he was here. We went back to HerringThope Leisure Centre on the bus and we did Archery I had a go but I had to be careful because I had it done for the first time on my chest it did hurt a bit but I was taking my time I was trying to aim it in the middle but I was missing it but at least I had a go. My friend said are you ok I said yes and he told me to take my time Anthony wasn't happy he didn't say anything to me. I think he woke up on the wrong side of the bed because he doesn't even smile. He didn't respect me and he was quiet and looked very anger. We went to Rotherham Football were the players go and had a tour then we had to go home or away and I went in away then we went inside I saw Anthony holding the same persons hand when we was In Meadowhall to finished the tour and my friend said its all over "it is now" I laugh with her and my ex partner didn't appreciate it that I was giggling too. We also went to Rotherham we went into a pub which was

Chapter 6

called Bluecoat JD Wetherspoon and we was playing pool and my uncle was in there with his mates I asked from a distance how does he know me I was he's niece, I wanted to go and speak to him but Anthony wouldn't let me I went into the toilet and started crying because I heard them talk about me and then I came back out and saw Anthony holding my friends hand which he was two timing me because I had a scar on my chest. He then let go of her hand and tried to do it again but I watch I should of said it's over. He supposed to be going out with me he rise his arm thinking he respects people when he doesn't and one of my uncle friends wanted me to go over I was trying to but my ex partner said I wouldn't dare. I felt traumatised and I felt I was to blame in the relationship because I can't speak to anyone or my uncle who I knew he's my family. I couldn't seem to get my control back the happy me. All I could think about is looking at my uncle wanted to go over and have a cuddle with him because that makes me feel calm. Me and my family went to the pub one weekend it was the Yellow Lion and I saw my uncle there with his friends I had Goosebumps and I asked him while I was sat down why I had them he said it's my and his presents. He did ask to see if I was alright I say yes but I could have asked to see why I had them. We went to a football ground I was having the best day ever wasn't all please that I

was having a laugh and a joke. We also went to see blood brothers that was amazing but made me jump at the end I didn't expect it. It also made my friend jump who was sat next to me on my right I also checked on my ex partner when we got back in the minibus and he raised his arm with a fist I think it made him jump too, we all didn't expect it we got back to college it was night time and we all went home I gave my ex partner a cuddle then went home. I was having fun as you do with your friends but then at college when I was cooking a Christmas cake with baileys in and I even tried a little bit because I haven't had it Baileys before and my ex partner didn't like it that I tried it. I could see it on his face that he didn't appreciate I was having some I don't know why he wasn't happy, when was putting the cake away he didn't like it very much because my other friends was laughing and joking and told me not to drop it which I didn't; then it was break time we all went our different ways and I got cornered by my ex partner he said that I told him that I had the operation and I was on tablets. I told him I hadn't had it before because had heart murmur he didn't think I wasn't aloud it because he thought I was On tablets and I told him I didn't have the operation because the hole was to big they couldn't do it, he was twisting my words and I called him manipulative. He wasn't happy that I even tried Baileys and the way I was taking the cake to the other side of the room and wanted to get away from him. He stop me from going to see my friends he corned me and I jumped. He wasn't happy when he got into College Anthony didn't tell me why he wasn't happy and I got slapped across the face. I was crying my eyes out I got a red mark around my left face two of my friends saw me crying where the toilets are and came up to me so I was walking around the college with two of my friends and told them what had happened I went into the canteen and walked straight passed him, I didn't want to look at him. Then we went to tell the teacher and then I had to go to another room because they had to speak with him and he had to leave which he got kicked out. I went back in the room and my friend said am I alright I said yes but all I could think about was the slap. I was trying to hide my tears but I was still upset and shacking the teacher said do you want us to take you home or do you want to go with your friends to take you to the bus station with my friends, I said I will go to the bus station with my friends and holder my friends arm and they was trying to make me laugh again. And I was laughing with them and also I was looking over my shoulder to make sure he wasn't there even at the bus stop.

I got to the bus station and went home. When I got home I sat down on the sofa trying not to get myself upset again and my dad wanted to talk to me and I went to him sat on his knee and told him and started crying again. My ex partner rang the house phone which I didn't answer it was my dad. I didn't see him until we went passed a classroom with his dad and Nannan. We didn't know that he was coming back in until I spotted him in a classroom. So I walked back to my friend and hug her then I walked out next to my friends. He wanted me to give him a hug outside of the college didn't want a hug from him but my friend said no and I didn't do it I walked away because I was still shocked by it I didn't want to talk to him anymore. Then on Monday he was coming back to college I think he was waiting for me. I didn't know he was doing it all I wanted him to do is to leave me alone and let me have my space he wasn't in a good mood he didn't even smile. I didn't go near him my heart was beating fast and one day when we was finished he was down the end of the path way I stop and looked at him my friend was calling him a woman beater which was true; I was scared because I thought I was going to get hit me again and I was going to cry again which I held back in me I didn't want him near me. I did have Goosebumps on me. We had to go in the minibus to go to the bus station I didn't want him to follow me nor talk to him. My friends were having a laugh and I wasn't I was still upset inside I wanted to cry but I hold the tears back then my bus came and I

Chapter 7

got on it my heart was racing I was trying to calm down I did see my uncle again, I was on the bus my heart was hurting but I was breathing normal to get it to calm down. And then a week later we went to Butlins in 2003 for a week and yes Anthony was ringing me asking me if I was alright he wouldn't leave me alone. I told him I wasn't interested in him anymore. We also went to see how beer was made yes I did take my phone which I should have left it in the department and I said I was in a lesson and he wouldn't listen. "Why did he ring when I wasn't there in college " and I said bye, but he was still ringing me but I didn't answer it I was ignoring it. I wanted to learn how beer was made. My ex partner was text me to see if I had a boyfriend it would have been my worst nightmare and wanted to know where I was but I didn't tell him I just wanted space. When we were coming back to the sky pavilion I saw the Wrestling was there which I missed; And he was still ringing me and I was still crying so told him to leave me alone which he wasn't doing. I was Upset and I didn't want to speak to him he wouldn't leave me alone. Wish I had watch it because I could of seen the Undertaker again wrestling but I looked and there he was my favourite wrestler of all times even the Butlin's Undertaker wanted to speak with me I didn't go near him I didn't tell my ex partner that he wanted to speak with me. He told me that I couldn't go on the rides when we was at Butlins I was trying to hold my tears back but I couldn't. I wished I had told my uncle which I saw in Butlins with his mates. We also went to visit our tutors sisters house when we was there but I didn't tell that to my ex partner, then we went back to college on the Friday and my ex partner was there outside the college where the gates were, I didn't know he was waiting there until I saw him. And then I had to have my operation for my heart murmur on the Monday I think I was in there for 5 days I was in intensive care after the operation I had tubes in me and I was asleep when they was doing it. I should of woken up about 1pm but I didn't wake up until about 5pm then I went back to the ward and rested my family Anthony wanted to visit me in hospital in Leeds but I didn't want him to come because I didn't want him to be upset or angry I didn't want him near me. I didn't have my phone with me because I couldn't. I was trying my hardest to keep my eyes open I was on tablets I was in pain I was there until they was happy with me to go home I did walk around the ward to help me get my routine I did cry because I wanted my own bed but I was there to get better and came back out on the Friday I couldn't go out because I was in pain and then they was a knock at the door my dad answered it and I went to the door and it was my ex partner came with his sister and with the dog he asked me to see if I could go out and I said no because I was too much in pain and I had to rest to let it heal. My heart was telling me one thing and my head was telling me another. And that didn't work. But if I could turn back the clock I would have talked to the Undertaker in Butlin's. Now I have two favourite wrestlers one in America and I haven't spoken to him either and one in Butlin's which I haven't spoken to yet. I didn't say much because I was on the phone to Anthony which he was making me upset, All I ever wanted is respect. I didn't say hi to Undertaker but wish I could and had his autograph and to tell him that he's an amazing wrestler which I will do one day, which will come true fingers crossed. One day I would love to go to Butlin's and see him again and this time I will get a book and his autograph. I would love to get to know him better and me his friend and fan of course, but still going to be a creature of the night for him, I'm never going to be scared of him even if I get goosebumps when his music comes on. I will always call that excitement day because I'm happy for him to come out and cheer him on; I always want him to win but if he lost I be proud of him that he has tried to do his best and that's all that matters. And the next day I went out I left it in the department and we went swimming I was enjoying myself and having fun. Me and my friend had a race and it was a draw and when I got back to the apartment that was it I wasn't in the best of moods, I tried to tell him Leave me alone but he wasn't listening he thought I had another boyfriend which I hadn't. He said if I had it be my worst nightmare. I wish I had now because I would have been better off without him in the first place. I was upset and told my friends what he said. I wish he was in a casket and let Him rot in hell. I wish I change my number before I went it would have been easier for me. He then asked why I haven't answered it, I said I was swimming because we chose to and to have so much fun. I was getting myself back and talking again because I didn't talk to me friends as much because what has happened to me. I had 13 missed calls from my ex partner he was paranoid I didn't know why he was ringing me because I wanted space and time to myself. He told me that I couldn't go on the rides when we was at Butlins He also said that I couldn't I had to do has he Said. He wanted to know everything what I was Up to even he said I had to do what he said. I told him is that a threat. But he was still ringing me but I didn't answer it until I got back in the mini bus he was upsetting me and wouldn't leave me alone, I asked him why aren't you leaving me alone because I had to do has he said is that a threat. At the end we had a presentation at college. I also got I also got 2 Essential Skills award 2003-2004. At that point he wanted to visit

Chapter 8

me in hospital in Leeds but I didn't want him to because I didn't want him to be upset or angry. I didn't have my phone with me because I couldn't. And that didn't work. When I return home I couldn't go out because I have to rest to get better. My dad answered the door and then I went to the door and it was Anthony with his dad, sister and the dog Anthony came to the house but not in the house and he wanted me to come out and I said no because I was in pain he saw the plaster on my chest it was white the air hit me has it does when you go out my heart was telling me one thing and my head was telling me another has he was going I went to the end of the street because that's how far I wanted to go, my heart was beating faster than normal I was breathing normal and it was calm. I should have listened to my Heart. I didn't listen to my mum and dad they tried their best to keep me away from him even my dad got bit by is dog on his back leg. I went back Home with my dad and my uncle I didn't want to be with him anymore because I was trying to tell him I didn't want a boyfriend anymore. We went to college and that's when he was holding anther persons hand because he knew I had I plaster on my chest and then he saw the scar I got kicked out. My ex partner told me that I couldn't see my family anymore nor my friends even said that I couldn't see a show with my two friends. I even heard downstairs that he was in control even the door was shut. He also said I had to cover my scar up because I knew I had to be careful because of the sun it was a nice day. I even put sun cream on but he wasn't having none of it. He even told me to change my vest top I couldn't where V tops or dresses, skirts or flip flops nor pumps or else. I couldn't get a tan.

We went to the seaside with his Nannan I was trying to keep my distance he was following me I couldn't go on the arcades he was raising his arm and telling me I had to do what he said. I wouldn't dare I had to do has he said. We also went into town and people was saying why are you holding your brother's hand when I knew I wasn't his brother but still people were thinking I'm his sister. I also saw my uncle and he wanted me to go to him which I didn't I wished I did I was trying too but my ex partner said I can't I wouldn't dare, and I told him from a distance. And that was the last time I went into town. I wish I went into town on my own because I would have been better to have been on my own because its easer. My ex partner told me not to but deodorant on I couldn't have high heels on or fails nails nor I couldn't where perfume nor nail varnish or jewellery, make up or have my hair drier or straightness, dyer my hair, cocktails simple which is another soap or wash my hair because there's no need to do it every week when your hair does get greasy. I couldn't watch DVD'S. I also don't like spiders and I got forced into holding one which I didn't want to do because my hands itch after which he didn't care I had to do what he said. One day I squashed one my accident I didn't know it was in the bedroom at the time until I got back from college. I never had a barbecue when I was with my ex partner or played anything in the garden of or had fish and chips or should I say batted sausage and chips. I never had fun when I was with him it felt like I was a different person like I was not a fun girl anymore like they was someone inside of my that I couldn't get out. When I was with my ex partner I couldn't go into town on my own without my ex partner or his sister and her dad. I went once to go to the doctors but I had goosebumps and I knew who it was but I didn't see him. I went to see my ex partner at work but couldn't see my uncle and talk to him my ex partner said I wouldn't dare. I couldn't Exercise has much all I was doing is walking or watch my soaps etc Coronation Street, EastEnders and Hollyoakes I couldn't have music on like Def Leppard, Thunder all the other music you listen too. or Wrestling WWE or do any word searches. I couldn't go out with my friends at night time. I also couldn't have steak, tuna,Pot Noodles salad bacon, BBQ sauce, coleslaw and relish. I missed them or Harry Potter or read to get better at my hard words. I couldn't iron my one clothes. I couldn't have ankle socks. All I was doing is sat in the bedroom doing nothing and thinking. I wasn't having fun like I did before I had a relationship. I Couldn't have chocolate nor the sweets because it rots your teeth, I had when I was younger only pringles. I couldn't have Curry's, pasta, cod in butter sauce chips, Eggs, waffles, alcohol, Walkers crips, mice, chicken, toasts, biscuits, cakes, flap jacks, ice cream, water, Fruit, orange juice, mushy peas, baked beans, mint sauce, meat and potato pie, pate, pepperoni, mushrooms, garlic Bread, sprits, wine, rice, jacket potato and a salad onions when you have Sunday lunch piccalilli, chicken, Chicken Nuggets, yogurt and sausages or to have smelly's in the bedroom or play games and the sauces what you have with your chips. I had liver that wasn't nice at all. I also couldn't have pizza I had to tell him when I am on my cycle he wasn't happy. I didn't have a app then because I didn't know when I was coming on or when I was ovulating. I even had sensitive skin which he didn't believe me. I even said that I don't like Apples with skin on but I still had to try it he was forcing me and then he was rising his fist he doesn't respect anyone. I went to Karate with my ex partner he wasn't happy that I wasn't doing it right that's why I wanted to go by myself and not with him I had to do has he said which I'm quite cable to go on my own when it had finished, they was people outside the co-op in sallowness which I didn't get involved they was banging on the bus saying why are you going out with your brother I just ignored it I will never be my ex partners sister am not an Algor I am a Biggin that what I was thinking in my head. I couldn't text my family has much and to see how they were I wanted to say hi to my mum but she went and he told me I had to do has he said and that upset me inside. I said to him I still had a family. Even when it was Halloween I couldn't go out and have fun I had to what he said even in a different character even if it was at the pub if they were doing it. I couldn't get any fresh air in me as much. He even did the ankle lock on me when you cant do it at home it does say PLEASE DON'T TRY THIS AT HOME!!!! He even rolled his eyes up because he thinks he's the Undertaker one day on the back garden when he's not he's not a professional wrestler he thinks I've got presents with him I told him that I haven't got presents with him when it's with my uncle who I knew. I couldn't go to the pub when we were going to the shop it was nighttime people was whistling at me. And asking me if I was alright which I knew I wasn't. I was trying to get away from him. We also went to the woods in Wickersley I saw my uncle he wanted me to go to him but I didn't wish I had because he would know what to do but my ex partner said I wouldn't dare I had to do has he said. One night we went to a friends house a friend went to get her boyfriend and I stayed there with her sister and my ex partner, they went to the bedroom without me and he started touching her where he shouldn't I started crying and walked in on them. I said your my boyfriend not hers and it's because I have a scar on my chest just because I have heart murmur with a scar on my chest doesn't mean you can disrespect me but he didn't listen she was shocked that I said that she

Chapter 9

thought he was single I couldn't believe my eyes. I should have said it was over but I was anger inside of me. I couldn't have beer I didn't have a drink because he was in control. I wanted a drink because my throat was dry his sister was and was ill I was sober. We had to go to hospital because she had taken something what she

shouldn't have then me and my ex partner
went home I went into the bedroom and sat on the
bed I wasn't happy with my ex partner because I
can have a drink my heart was fine I know my
body. I saw my uncle again I couldn't say hi to him
he was stopping me from doing that he said I
wouldn't dare he wasn't interested in him it was
me that he was interested in. I am his niece who I
have presences with it was going up and back
down again I didn't say anything I should have
gone and spoken to him he could have helped me.
I still don't know why I get them even now. My ex
partner also didn't appreciate that I was spending
time with my family I and not him. We never had
cuddles anymore they were no love there we
Didn't hold hands or said I love you to each other.
He wasn't interested I also should have gone to
my mum and dads for tea then I forgot then I did
the next day I went. heard him having a laugh and
joke with his dad I had new clothes and he didn't
appreciate that I had new clothes and telling
him that he was in control he didn't care and
that was indoors I wished I had a better phone
then I could of recorded it. I had a Nokia. I wished
id gone into town and had my space. I was ill
one day I had to go to the doctors because I
had constipation, My ex partner was out and
came home then my ex partner came in and did
what Goldberg did which you can't do. I was
scared of him it felt like I can't speak to anyone

anymore. I had medication to help me get better. They told me once a woman beater always a woman beater. I was looking for a job in Morthyng and I saw him holding anther girls hand and then he let go he supposed to be going out with me not going out with her too and that was in June 2005. I couldn't get one. Also I had to go home because I wasn't well, I had headache and I got myself some water my ex partner was upstairs and I was down starts and that day I didn't eat my tea because I wasn't hungry and I heard Anthony talking saying he didn't care. I was asleep on the sofa I woke up and saw my ex partner playing on the PlayStation but he was losing a game and wasn't in a good mood, it was only a game I didn't know Steve at that point. In September 2005 I went to Dinnington college the same one I met my ex partner and I met Steve Horncastle we was just friends at that point I was sat on my own until he said to sit with them. My ex partner was ringing me every 5 minutes I was ignoring it he was making sure I was fine and he told me he thought I wanted a job which I did but couldn't get one it was hard at that point. He also told me that he couldn't come to college after I finished lessons. I knew that was why I wanted to go back to college because that were I was safe at the time, because I knew when I finished I had two ways to get home. We got to know each other which was good to get to know other people then at brake time I went outside for some fresh air where the mini buses are and Steve offered me a cigarette and I said no thank you and then I went up to him and gave him a cuddle I but my head in his jacket. One day I got told not to go near Steve because we got told he hit someone and it wasn't true. Its only because I got slapped across the face and my ex partner got kicked out. I didn't tell my mum and dad until a week later but when I finished lessons I was scared to go back to him I knew I had the chance to go home to the people who loved me and respected me or go to my ex partner who didn't care anything about me. Me and my ex partner went out with his Cousin into town in his car I was at college at the time there were cars there with lights on the bottom of the cars like sports cars which was a Wednesday night and the club was open I have never been in there I saw my uncle there he didn't see me it was mine and my uncle presence and my ex partner doesn't respect me or called me nice words only respects himself even when it was Christmas. But that didn't stop there. I knew I had to get out of it but I didn't know how to get out of the relationship even I tried everything my confidence went downhill. I even told him to leave me alone but still ignoring me so I had to get the help and support somehow there. I couldn't go out as much as I wanted to, He was very controlling he told me that I'm ugly, not a princess, not a flower, not a pet, not beautiful and

all the other nice words people say even he said that I'm not allowed to where summer clothes and he told me I couldn't see my family and I didn't listen because I knew I had a family still. My ex partner even said that I had to have my hair cut short because he doesn't like long hair girls. I even went to get my bike but it had a flat tyre but I still went on it and my ex partner was still telling me I had to do has he said and I was crying again so I turned around. I saw my uncle with his mates he wasn't interested in my ex partner it
was me who he was interested in I should of gone near him and talk to him because he knows me more then my ex partner does because I'm his family but I didn't go near my uncle I was just talking to him and my ex partner didn't appreciate that I was talking to him he said that I had to do what he said and went back but not home which I should of done, I didn't know who I was anymore sometimes I wish I wasn't here but I knew in my heart I had a family that knows me more than anyone that's why I was keeping strong. I wish I had a nice phone then with pictures on it to look back on including when I was at a wedding that's a good memory. I even went to the seaside with him and he was still trying to control me. I just wanted to be me again I felt like I was somebody else inside of me that I couldn't get out of the situation I kept saying to myself that he's controlling me and I was scared of

Chapter 10

him but didn't say it I didn't know how to. I even wanted to say it was over because he wanted to two time me with another girl and that upset me. But did he care no he didn't want me. He just wanted me to be jealous of him because he was in control and that's how I knew. One night we went to the pub and I had a Cola Cola and he had a pint and whiskey he said two with his fingers so I said to the bar lady that he's controlling me he wasn't happy that I can talk to people or play darts I was taking my time I hadn't played darts before so I knew I had to take my time step by step. He had the right hump on I knew I can talk to people, then they were a fight outside I stayed in I didn't want to get involved people thought I was is sister when I wasn't. So we went home with his dad and cousin the bar lady said controller I knew who she meant I didn't get her name but I told him he's controlling as well, when we were going home. I knew I had a sister and a brother already that respect me yes we do argue but I'm still family and I knew I had a respectful family that knows me more than my ex partner ever did. One day me and my ex partner was arguing he then got his hands around my neck that was his dads place and I couldn't breathe and he hit me. I got hit in my left side the night before I thought I broken my ribs at one point because it was hard to breathe. I was very upset my ex partner came into the bedroom and he saw me he didn't care nor did his sister or dad no one checked on me I was shaking I was trying to call the police but I was shaking too much to do it. So I went downstairs to find my keys but couldn't so I could get some fresh air and go to the police station without them knowing I was going but couldn't find them. So I went to sleep and the next day my ex partner wasn't there he must have been at his cousin's place. The next day I went to college I was very upset and I was trying to find my keys and trying to but my coat on and my keys was in my coat and I went to college but wanted To get help but didn't know how long it was because I was so much in pain it wouldn't stop hurting. I got up tried to have my breakfast but it was really hurting and I was trying to breath normally but when I was doing so my side was hurting me so much I wanted to cry again which I was crying and trying not to so I was thinking to myself that's it, it's so over so I went to put my coat on I was struggling with it because of my lefted side was hurting when I was breathing in it hurts. I went out the door to the fresh air hit me. He said he had promised not to hurt me but that was a lie. I went to college I was crying my eyes out and I was trying to fight the tears back but couldn't and that was it I didn't want to go out with him anymore. What I should have done is gone to the police station and told them but I didn't know how long they was going to take because I had to go to college. And that was the final decision I have ever made. I should have been single when my ex partner got kicked out of college once a woman beater always will be he will never change. There were things going through my mind which I couldn't say. I even wanted to say it was over because he wanted to two time with another girl and that upset me, but "did he care no". He didn't want me. He just wanted me to be jealous of him because he was in control of me and that's how I knew I should of listen to my mum and dad because I had heart murmur because I have a scar on my chest 2 scars. My ex partner doesn't care for anyone but himself if he cared for a woman then he would have respected that I was seeing my family and going to see my friends which I hardly was seeing and going to college. I didn't go near Steve because I was upset my left side was hurting me I couldn't hardly breath I got hit by my ex partner and I told Steve I didn't want to go out with my ex partner anymore. I wanted to go out with Him and he dealt with it. I went to the house and got my things I saw him in his bedroom on the Bed because that's where I went before I left, he had a red face saying he was sorry he's never sorry he should of respected me or even talked to me I'm not a mind reader but I turned around and said you're not sorry. When you say no he gets the face on or when you laugh he doesn't appreciate it. I don't know what goes on inside his head. But I didn't care anymore the way he Treated me and He had no respect for me. I was still hurting but I didn't show it I was just holding my Left side to protected it. I just looked at him he Was mumbling and going red on his face and he was crying like a little boy. I think he was trying to say sorry but it was too late for apologies. If he cared that much he would have treated me with respect and my family and he would of listen to me and stop ringing me when I had a break at Butlin's. All he cares about was himself not me. But he doesn't even know what respect is and now I know once a woman beater always will be. He will never change even though he said he had and it was a promise and he lied to me. Now I understand why they were trying to keep me safe. I was happy that Steve sorted it out for me. Steve told my why he was in college and the reason why he was in bracken he was having problems and he walked away from it. I had to have a operation on my heart I told Steve that I was going to hospital but I couldn't have my phone and that's 2007. I couldn't talk to Steve but dad was with me to talk to him so he can get the updates and he respects me. We were engaged by then he got down on 1 knee and he proposed to me and I said yes. He came to visit me in hospital I was trying to keep my Eyes open. Then I said where's Steve He then Said he's holding your hand then I had a big Smile on my face. I was on morphine which was a pain relief because last time I was on tablets which was working a bit but not a lot. Me and Steve Went on our first date it

Chapter 11

was his best man wedding that was a good day and night. I was also working at that point which I enjoy. I also did Kick Boxing for a bit that was good too I haven't used that on anyone. We also went to the pub together I was quite and then I got my confidence and now I'm talking more than ever now. There's more to come in our future. WE have also been to Benidorm which is nice to get away for a bit nice area and very hot too. We do argue but we stick by each other. And now I am still having it hard. I have also had a injection which is called pneumonia I've had my Uncle that was an alcoholic and it started when I was 18/19years old. I've witnessed it. I have been to hospital & visit him with the family it was very hard because I thought he was getting better but it turn out it wasn't. I saw my Auntie there with her two children when they was younger. And I told Steve I was visiting him in hospital so I would ring him after when I got back. Also when this was going off with my Uncle, my Nannan Biggin was diagnosed with cancer and it was breast cancer. My Nannan Biggin wanted to meet Steve and do him spaghetti Bolognaise. I didn't know what food Steve liked at the time I didn't asked him. But now I know he likes it. I was in the village at the time at the weekend and before that my Nannan Biggin was in hospital so I still went with Steve to enjoy the weekend. I rang my sister to see if Nannan Biggin was alright on the Saturday and my sister was very upset Nannan passed away on the Friday in hospital and she also had pneumonia which it spread too. she told me not to cry but I couldn't help but cry with her on the phone. My sister also said that she's with Uncle David which was my dads brother and the family's too who had brain tumour just remember that, and I said ok if Nannan Biggin was here I would of told her that he likes spaghetti Bolognaise. I was 20 years old when Nannan passed away. Steve didn't come with me because he didn't know her. But he was there to support me, he even gave me two boxing gloves and every time I wanted to be upset I did cry and I couldn't stop crying and I holded my them that was heartbreaking for us all I was crying all the way though and having chills going up my spine I also had goosebumps on my arms I don't know how that happened all I was saying is where's my uncle I wish he had been there I saw my cousins and I had a cuddle with the oldest one.

I told her I miss her its not going to be the same without her and she said remember the good times and I said I will try, so I gave my other cousins a hug but they didn't come for a drink afterwards. I didn't want her to go. I was very upset about it and even kept that under my chin. I miss her every day and I will never disrespect her. My uncle came back to his mum's house after the funeral I knew I had the chance to talk to him, I knew I was still young, but it was my decision, it was Mine and his presences again. I don't know why he was coming back but I wish I found out because it makes sense why he was coming back. I wish I had contact with him because I do miss him and I do think about him he's still family. I've got photos to look back on and remember the good times it's not the same without contact It's better to keep in touch with him and to make sure he's fine. And also when I was 21years old my uncle didn't come to my birthday party. It was just my Auntie that came to my birthday party and the rest of the family and that's a year after my Nannan passed away in 2005. When I get married in 2010 and moved Steve works as a lorry driver and I work too I've also done my certificates Frist Aid, Moving and Handling, Safeguarding, Pear & Pear Abuse, Asthma Awareness, Basics British sound language, CPR & Defibrillator Awareness, COSHH, Open Learning children's perspectives on play, Financial accounting and reporting, Intermediate Italian: Describing people Vocabulary in Italian Infants understanding of their social world, Beginners Italian: Food and drink, Allergywise, Safeguarding Children with Special Educational needs and Disabilities, onlinefirstaid Choking and Suicide Awareness and Pervention, Dealing with Bereavement and Loss, An Introduction to the General Data Protection Regulation. But still keep in touch with my family and friends, my Uncle what was an alcoholic rang me at midnight one weekend and when I was asleep but I answered it because he wanted to talk to me. He wanted to meet up with me on a Thursday but I couldn't because I was working and it sounded like he was drinking because he forgot Steve name he was on night then and when we finished our conversation I cried myself to sleep and he's met him before, my Grandad Biggin passed away in hospital in 2013 I've never disrespected him nor disrespected my family and I will never do a few days later and about 2014/2015 my Uncle Died and it was burst appendix. I know what an alcoholism is because I have witnessed it, next door was the same and it is challenging at times. I just what people to understand not to criticise people that haven't been in that same situation until they have witnessed it themselves. I also have seen bands with my dad, Sarah (step mum) and Steve in Rotherham, Barnsley, Sheffield and I've

Chapter 12

also seen my uncle who I have presents with chills going up my spine and down again with his mates and I've see my mates in Maltby and I've seen him there too. Also in Doncaster. I have also had presence when I was going to my Aunties and uncles house in WoodSeats going passed my Nannan and Grandad old street not gone down it but I knew where my Nannan and Grandad live at the time when I was younger I've never accused anyone in my life and I will never say that word. And I've never disrespected anyone in my family. But I know that I have been accused of saying it without people mentioning it first. When I've been through it again from 2019 2021. It is upsetting and stressful because I can't believe that when I try and say it without getting upset people don't believe me. Instead I get accused of saying it when I haven't accused someone like that, that hasn't said it first. I do get upset about it people may not be in that position. I want to talk about it and get people to be aware that alcohol is poisonous. I know we all like a drink but we know our limits. Whatever happened to being kind. You don't know what people are going through in their lives. Why did it say last year Britain get talking on Britain's got talent on TV. It could be anything you want to talk about but just remember not to accuse someone. Just listen to what they have to say and ask them to see if they need that help and support them in the hard times. I have also had a injection which is called pneumonia and a heath check up. I also went to Chatsworth with my mum and Nannan Nichols for the day. I also we went to two weddings this year 2023.

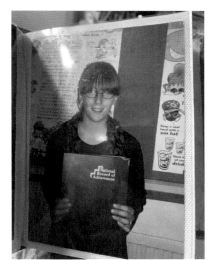

Printed in Great Britain
by Amazon

33564386R00041